Eve Was a Realist

Poems for the Untamed Heart

Fiona Robertson

Gawthorne Press

Copyright © Fiona Robertson 2024
The moral rights of the author have been asserted.

Published in the United Kingdom by Gawthorne Press
Unit 18519, PO Box 7169, Poole, BH15 9EL

All rights reserved. No part of this book may be reproduced by any mechanical, photographic or electronic process, or in the form of a phonographic recording, nor may be stored in a retrieval system, transmitted or otherwise copied for public or private use, other than for 'fair use' as brief quotations embodied in articles and reviews, without the prior written permission of the publisher.

ISBN 978-1-9164686-3-4

Cover art copyright © Nikki England
Cover design by Adam Mckillop

British Library Cataloguing-in-Publication Data
A catalogue record for this book is available from the British Library

Fiona Robertson's poems are love letters to our humanity and our efforts to understand what it means to know ourselves as both the great mystery and the big brave work of embodiment. I feel deep gratitude that she has expressed her journey in this way and has shared it with us.

C. Abigail Pingree, author of *Completion: A Memoir*

Throughout these pages, Fiona Robertson invites the reader to reside in the intimacy of her exquisite, deeply personal and simultaneously transrational unfolding. We are guided into the liminal space between the known and the unknown – into the gap between thoughts – to join a kindred soul in a sustainable shared inquiry. "In this mystical space, intellectual reasoning flounders and linear time veers off its tracks." Fiona's words sing like windchimes!

Rashani Réa
Artist, earth steward and farmer, and author of forty books of art and poetry, including *Beyond Brokenness* and *Beneath All Appearances: an unwavering peace*

Contents

Preface 1
Bittersweet 4
Falling 6
Barking Up the Wrong Tree 7
When You Wish It Were Not So 9
Iconoclasm 11
The Stunning Symmetry of Opposites 12
We Are Land 13
This Silent Vow 14
When You Let Life In 15
It Is Not Necessary 16
Body 17
Come Back to The Well 18
This Is an All-Inclusive Ticket 19
These Books and I 20
There's Nothing Wrong Here 21
Life Has No Need of Happy Endings 22
Not a Hair's Breadth 23
Making Something of It 24
I Am Not the Author 25
The World 26

Selling Yourself Short	27
The Ballad of Me	28
Even This	29
This Is What No One Can Teach	30
For All Those Who Have Been Humiliated	31
Check The Small Print	32
The Second Coming	33
Eve Was a Realist	34
This Is What Love Does	35
In The Museum of Suffering	36
I Beg to Differ	37
Epithets	38
Sunken	39
No Further Instruction	40
Aftermath	41
Muddying the Water	42
Wild	43
Inhibition	44
I Am All That	46
Such Is Grace	47
Instinct	48
All That Matters	49
Life Will Move Me	50
There Is Nothing To Be Done	51

Butterflies Do Not Condemn Caterpillars 52
On Sunday Afternoon 54
Let the Silence Descend 55
Here's The Miracle 56
As If All There Is Isn't Enough 58
Quietism 59
When Love Comes Home 60
The Time Will Come 61
Dare You Be So Bold? 62
Utterances 63
Devotion 64
Pandora 65
Beneath Blood and Bone 66
Wherewithal 68
Acknowledgements 71
About the Author 72

Preface

I am a slow poet. Slow, because I am the opposite of prolific. Slow, because I only began writing poetry in my early fifties. Slow, because the writing of these poems happens at its own pace, a pace I can do nothing to alter. I have come to marvel, in fact, at the tidal nature of the process, how in those rare moments the flow begins and all I need do is be there with pen in hand.

Poems come solely when I am in the space of what might very loosely be called inquiry. In this space, I am un-scrutinised and un-scrutinising, allowing all my experience to be as it is. An organic unfolding ensues, which inevitably moves in unforeseeable ways; all the poems in this collection emerged during such moments. They are artefacts of dynamic, embodied experience rather than declarations of arrival or finality.

When I am willing to fall into the truth of my inner experience such as it is in each moment – often a far cry from what I might wish it to be or what I am attempting to make it – there is an unravelling of psychological and somatic patterns, and a spontaneous excavation of the sedimentary layers of self and world. It is a space in which things make themselves known, express, dissolve, tell their truth, evolve, regress, mend, radiate, or fall away. Here, I come to know myself as – and have the felt experience of being – a plurality, rather than the singular self that I usually take myself to be. Voices seemingly other than my own, yet intimately a part of me, begin to speak. Whether the voices that emerge are from body, psyche, or soul; past, present, or future; the personal, collective, or archetypal; or the divine or universal, their words are inevitably unexpected, often counterintuitive, and sometimes even shocking.

In this mystical space, intellectual reasoning flounders and linear time veers off its tracks. Those of us who explore this terrain – I know I am far from being the only one – often find ourselves in states of excruciating pain, heartbreaking beauty, or profound revelation. This is where we meet love – or god, if you prefer – and come to know ourselves as *this* as well as *that*. This is where we discover that what seems so broken is simultaneously wholly intact. More than anything else, it is in this intensely personal and private space that we discover what it is to be in the never-ending process of becoming fully human, of maturing into ourselves in the deepest of ways.

Paradox resides here in this space between the known and the unknown. Here, at the edge of unfolding, the polarity of either/or that has been so comprehensively embedded in us individually and collectively (I speak as someone born and educated into the dominant cultural paradigm) becomes both/and or, more precisely, and/and/and *ad infinitum*. It is a place of both stunning simplicity and unknowable complexity. Our usual ways of perceiving and conceiving no longer apply. Temporarily, we are moved out of our normal mode of being and into something more real, more alive, because here, nothing is cut off or excluded, one thing is not favoured over another, and things are not at all as we thought they were. Here, we get to see who we really are, unmired by the layers of conditioning in which we are usually swathed.

Over time, as we return to this space over and over again, we find ourselves, like Eve, discovering the illusory nature of our Edens. There are moments of devastating disillusionment and disappointment as the monuments we have built and the idols we have worshipped crumble. By turns, we fall into or out of states and feelings that we've desperately tried to deny the existence of or equally desperately hung onto. It is a profound and alchemical process, a distillation of our selves. The previously unseen makes its way from the depths to the surface, from the shadows to the light. Moments of realisation and insight emerge from the dross of this exploration, and point the way forward moment by moment. We gradually become more aligned with reality, and a little saner.

It can be hard, in current times, to find the space and time to sink into ourselves. Space and time are, in themselves, something of a luxury, and yet many of us find ourselves with no choice but to yield to the sinking. This collection is dedicated to everyone who is in this terrain; to everyone who is sinking, crumbling, falling, dissolving, opening, evolving, realising; to everyone who is on this journey into the depths of their humanness and discovering the pain and preciousness therein.

Bittersweet

I bathe in the bittersweetness
of ill sons
and bereaved friends
and strangers connecting
and and and

old friends back on track
and death in life
and birth after death
and the limitations of language
and the beauty of words
and pain with depth
and the realness of me

and all this turning upside down
and creation from destruction
and *who'd have thought it*
and *I wouldn't have guessed*
and we know so much
and we know so little.

And the bittersweetness
sits in my heart
and pulls at my heartstrings
(you know we have heartstrings)
and I'm in love with it all
and I wouldn't want anything less
and I'm not looking for anything more.

I bathe in bittersweetness,
that tang in the heart
that leaves nothing to do
and nowhere to go
and the tears run down my cheeks
and one drops from the end of my nose
and I can't pretend that I don't love it all
and that this isn't what my heart was made for.

Falling

Always scared of falling,
I clung on, holding fast
to anything that seemed secure.

Eventually, it all gave way
and I dangled, desperately bracing
against the inevitable screaming descent
of my solid body to the ground.

Finally, I jumped
(having exhausted every other option)
but instead of the expected terrifying hurtle,
I was caught by a gentle upward draught.

Stunned, I discovered my weightlessness
and the total absence of places to land:
all further struggle rendered unnecessary.

Barking Up the Wrong Tree

You've been barking up the wrong tree.

You think you want out of this
but what you most long for
is to be right in it.

You think you want it all to stop
yet what you're yearning for
is the start.

You think you're afraid to die.
In truth, you're afraid to live,
scared witless by your untamed aliveness.

You think you want love to make you whole
when really what your heart most wants
is for love to take you apart
so you can taste the sweet fruits of annihilation.

You think you should keep it all together
but your true longing
is for it all to fall apart
so catastrophically that you'll be left with nothing
and the game will be over.

I know, I know –
it all got so horribly complicated
and you thought that's what life was.

Trust me –
seeing the simplicity of this
will take your breath away.

When You Wish It Were Not So

You wish to fashion life,
to carve it according to your desires.
At times, you sculpt carefully, delicately;
a corner rounded off here,
an edge whittled away there,
seemingly without violence.

More often, your cuts are
swifter, frantic, more desperate,
as you hack away at everything
you wish were not so.

Despite your efforts to excise
all that you dislike,
life – whilst it may at first appear
to conform to your will –
has a tendency to remain
stubbornly, brazenly whole.

It keeps all those discarded,
broken, misshapen pieces for you,
knowing that one day you will need them.
They are essential to your survival,
for they are the very thing
your soul most craves.

Then, when all the defences
have been stripped away,
when not a single sinew is left

to hold you upright,
when struggle, effort and opposition
are ablaze on the pyre,
and you are prepared to fall
on the sword of what was
and what wasn't –

you'll realise there was never
anything missing.
Despite this loss
of incalculable proportions –
all is intact. You're whole. You're here.

Iconoclasm

Body and soul were cleft,
cathedrals built on the bones of women
and wombs made unclean;
creation stemmed and stymied
by the sheer pain of denying
that flesh *is* spirit.

We went from true communion among us
to looking up to some *idea* of god.

It is not that
you are not your body,
for your body is
the most sublime creation
of what you are,
creativity made flesh
so that it may create,
your constant companion
through all your travails,
the bearer of your sorrows.

Worship not god
but hand, eye, foot, breast –
the true bringers
of love and sustenance.
Dismantle your temples and shrines,
make your icons ordinary,
tend to the divine in your midst.
This wound runs deep in us all.

The Stunning Symmetry of Opposites

I thought this wasn't enough.

I wasn't terrified of death.
I was terrified this was all there was.
I was terrified life might only be this.
I was trying to survive on one shore
despite the waves
carrying me relentlessly
to the other.

I didn't understand –
it's enough
just to be here.

Today, I can't find a difference
between life and death.
Life completes death,
death completes life.
There's black's velvet comfort,
white's deep delight.
The staggering completeness of it all –
the stunning symmetry of opposites.

We Are Land

This is not the time to break.

Much as I long for
the refuge of the waters,
the headlong dive into brokenness,
we are made of stone, too,
and can contain all that flows.
Holding our shape,
the granite of our bones
such a necessary strength,
if we're to avoid a drowning.

Mammals of land and sea,
shallow, deep,
liquid and solid,
we are beyond yet needful of both,
as dependent on one as the other.

Study the charts:
sometimes it's wiser
to answer the Sirens' call
and bask on the rocks a while,
the wind and sun drying our skin,
our contours once again defined.

The depths will reclaim us
soon enough.

This Silent Vow

With no thought to any *ought*,
I do just what's required.
The absence of rules,
observances and resolutions
brings a deeper resolve,
a wordless commitment:
to meet whatever calls.

No longer
abandoning abandonment,
fearing fear,
rejecting rejection
or leaving loneliness on its own:
to dwell in abandoning, fearing,
and rejecting until
their time is done.

This silent vow
is to be here for it all.
To consecrate the mundane,
to see the worldly in the divine.
To move my allegiance from those false idols –
what wasn't and what may yet be –
to worship at the altar of what is.
To stand naked and vulnerable,
no longer sheltering
in the shade of beliefs or excuses,
to emerge into the light of now,
blinking and a little timidly, at first.

When You Let Life In

When you're willing to give
every single last thing –

you'll give up your bargaining,
your frantic insisting,
you'll disband the border controls,
dismantle the surveillance
and you'll stop counting life
in units of you.

When you let life in
the door will open
and everything will hurt
so much –
that you'll laugh helplessly.

Open the door to love,
and pain will come too.
Open the door to pain,
and love will inevitably
follow.

It Is Not Necessary

It is not necessary
to demean yourself
or to dramatize
your life.
(You are not a fiction,
and neither am I.)

The proliferation of *things*
has brought us scant riches.

I grieve for
the poverty in plenty,
for the ignorance
in knowledge.

Our souls
do not long for complication.
True nourishment
is simple fare:
taste, touch, smell,
sound, sight.

The heart loves,
the mind thinks,
the stomach digests.
You are the perfect orchestration
of being, an instrument of wonder.

It is not necessary to demean yourself.

Body

And my body says:

there's a fucking cosmos in here –
suns stars galaxies comets –
you should know
I am so much more than

a storehouse for your trauma or
a battleground for your conflicts or
the bearer of your scars or
the carrier of your soul
so don't pull your reductive objectifying imperialist
bullshit on me.

I am not something to be colonised by
whatever good intentions you have this month
or your warped ideas
about purity and perfection.

Let's just say
I know all your sleights-of-hand,
your baiting and switching.
We both know who you are
and we both know that you should be
on your knees, sinking into me,
worshipping at my feet,
and howling at my very miraculousness.

Come Back to The Well

Come back to the well,
and quench your thirst
for aliveness.

Rage with the torrents.
Spin with the whirlpools.
Pause in the millpond stillness –
all of it water, however it flows.

Jump right in –
you'll get wet, of course,
you might even risk a soaking –
but why make do with the sidelines of life?

Marvel at the miracle
of your imagining.
Revel in your maddest thoughts,
your most insane notions.
Rejoice in your body's contortions,
the aches of the flesh.

You see and are seen.
You do and are done unto.
You hear and are heard.
You act and are acted upon.
You know, are known,
and are the knowing of it all.

Why pretend you're anything but?

This Is an All-Inclusive Ticket

Believing yourself unworthy,
deeply flawed, incomplete,
you deny your total acceptability.

When you read the small print, you'll see:
this is an all-inclusive ticket
with no caveats,
exclusions or conditions.
There is nothing to dispose of,
box up or pack away.

The price of admission covers everything:
no further payments are required.

These Books and I

The books on these shelves here –
once laden with promise,
heavy with the hope of salvation –
no longer groan
under the weight
of such responsibility.

I supped greedily on their words,
desperately praying that the pages
might magically convey
the nectar of freedom
to transmute my undoubted suffering.

Surely, I reasoned,
the answer must reside
somewhere in those sentences?

I glanced across at them tonight,
familiar words on their spines,
and their colours against
the white of the bookcase,
offering nothing,
no longer required to hold out hope,
and relieved of the burden
of redeeming me.

There's Nothing Wrong Here

There's nothing wrong here.
Yes, I'm hurt,
but that's the point –
to break open, to give up,
to lay down my weapons,
plans, strategies, objections –
to finally say yes.

All I need do is see
and I'm already seeing.

God is this floor
and this tune
and this cushion
and this nearly-cold tea
this pen
this hand
this breath.

The separation was never separate.
The fading was always in full view.
I have exhausted myself going
precisely nowhere.

Life Has No Need of Happy Endings

All life wants is to know itself –
to know and to be known,
to be seen, touched, sensed, experienced.

Life has no need of happy endings:
when you drop your demand
for it to please you,
when you're no longer screaming
for it to make you happy,
it unashamedly delights in itself,
in its own sheer miraculousness.

Life sends forth its invitation
to you every day and you,
making your myriad excuses,
usually decline because
you know that if you say yes,
your very own ten thousand things,
your wonderful, labyrinthine creations
will lose their substance,
their gravity, around which
you revolve.

Once you finally stop spinning -
you will see that all life is here,
and unadorned, sublime,
it truly has no need of
happy endings.

Not a Hair's Breadth

We're trying to be
what we already are –
striving to mend the unbroken –
now there's a thankless task.

Yes, I know it feels
as if we're shattered,
flawed, in need of ministration,
yet complete and incomplete
have not a hair's breadth
between them.

Trust me – you are
as miraculous today
as you were on the day
you were born.

Making Something of It

The story, barely begun,
meets silence today –
a change from
the customary
making something of it.

No momentum forward,
no pull back.
Bemused by the lack of movement,
I sit and do nothing,
the aliveness of my senses
wholly apparent.

A question: *what is here?*
The answer beyond comprehension,
yet known nonetheless.

What if I object to nothing,
and things are as they are?

I Am Not the Author

I am not the author of this play:
defying all my attempts to rewrite,
recast, edit or expunge,
each scene has remained
stubbornly true to itself
knowing that I,
despite my protestations,
have no idea
how the script is written.

Neither am I the architect of this house:
its arcs, lines and curves,
its walls and doors,
none are of my making.
Whatever my claims,
life's form is entirely its own.

(Oh, the sweet futility of wanting to make alterations to
a design the intricacies and hues of which leave me
open-mouthed and speechless with gratitude.)

The World

It's so much simpler than I think:
there's nothing to monitor,
evaluate, control, compare,
and there's nothing to save or lose.

There's only one coin,
despite my ability
to see both sides.

Those grand opposites –
life and death,
better or worse,
up or down –
no longer holding sway.

How much I've longed
to be back here,
where being has no opposite,
where there is endless space
in which to meet it all.

Selling Yourself Short

My guess is
you're trying to not be
what you are –
so wonderfully, hysterically futile.

My guess is
you're selling yourself
woefully short –
I know I did.

I kept my sights in check,
punched well below my weight,
procrastinated, dissembled
and came up with a hundred excuses,
believing that if I hid beneath the parapet
I might escape the inescapable.

Trying not to be this made me mad –
not all-out bonkers insane but
contained, constrained, numb.

Then the lying came to an abrupt halt.
There was I, totally exposed,
deeply insecure, stumbling uncertainly,
rendered utterly incapable of being anything
other than this, here, now –
and inexplicably, incomprehensibly happy.

The Ballad of Me

I tried not to feel it
yet not feeling it was so much
more painful than feeling it.

I tried not to need, thinking
that if I could not need
I'd get what I needed.

I knew this wasn't it
and I ignored that knowing
in all the ways I knew how.

Intent on proving myself right,
I waited (in vain)
for you to validate
my version of me.

I built a shrine to myself.
I sang the ballad of me.

Even This

I'll admit it:

I'm really fucking scared
(well, life can be terrifying) –

and there was I
trying so hard
to not be scared,
whining and cajoling,
debating, bargaining, pleading:
Not this, surely not this.

Life didn't give in
so I get to see
I can admit
even this.

Even this.

This Is What No One Can Teach

No one ever taught me how to feel this pain.
I learnt how to doubt and second guess myself
so all this time, I've been stopping well short.

I no longer want your promises of salvation –
such an inadvertent disservice,
such a well-intentioned unkindness.

No one ever taught me how to lay myself open.

But what greater freedom is there than to feel this,
thus rendering everything else –
having served its purpose –
null and void?

My body, arcing and shaking,
finally dances to its own tune.

Numerous are the temptations to avoid this desert.
Many are the whispers to stay away,
to be unfaithful to ourselves.

This is what no one can teach.

For All Those Who Have Been Humiliated

I've been holding out, believing
that patience is a virtue
when, in truth,
I am beyond frustration.

To save you from the offence
of having to take me as I am
I died a little every day.

Toned myself down,
made myself smaller,
dulled it all a little.
No stride, no demands.
I went underground
thinking I'd find solace
in the subterranean depths.

Except:
this cannot be
contained or constrained,
nor should it be.
This is what no one could see.
This is what was hidden.

Out in the daylight now,
blinking hesitantly
yet breathing much more easily,
I'm thankful.

Check The Small Print

This territory I'd staked out,
in the mistaken belief
that it was mine;
when I checked the small print
I discovered it doesn't belong to me,
however vehement my claims.

I demanded conditionality,
preferring confinement to the expanses beyond.
I kept accounts; favours done, debts incurred,
all weighed in the balance
as I exacted my imagined dues.

I thought life owed me,
and I thought you did, too.

I've bled myself dry
trying to make life abide
by my caveats,
clauses and conditions.

Without them,
I am so outrageously,
indecently alive.

The Second Coming

The meek shall inherit the earth.

Quake in your boots
those who presume
on the souls or
bodies of others;
those who assume
title, rank or reign;
those who betray
heart-filled goodness;
and those who sunder
the flesh of innocents
to feed the maws of greed –
such vile, violent treason.

Quake in your boots.
The meek are rising
to reclaim the earth:
this is the second coming.

Eve Was a Realist

I feigned ignorance
until that first touch –
but mercifully,
my spell in Eden was brief.

I tumbled from the garden
bruised but ever-grateful
that we can't unknow
what we know.

Surely we've all bitten into the apple
a little too eagerly at times,
intent on proving our innocence?

Eve was a realist.
She knew it was time
to blow the whistle
on all Adam's fig-leaf cover ups,
and like all good messengers,
she got shot.

In the silence, I hear her whisper:
Tree or no tree,
you already know how naked you are,
so stop pretending otherwise.

This Is What Love Does

The talismanic thinking,
the hedging of bets,
each carefully tended plan,
every last strategy,
all previously struck deals and bargains:
love took them all
out of my hands today
and I – willingly this time –
gave them all up to love.

This is what love does
so we can pass through
the needle's eye
and enter the kingdom
of the heaven
we thought was elsewhere.

In The Museum of Suffering

My carefully curated collection
has been well-tended, as has yours:
we stayed with the cross
long after Christ himself
had ascended into heaven,
our suffering selves
sanctified and idolised,
the supposed meaning of his death
lost on us.

Do not make
a special case for suffering:
those velvet-bound exhibits
in their glass cabinets,
however precious,
do not confer nobility
nor special blessings.
(I believed my soul would profit,
but that was a lie.)

We fetishised the cross,
and postponed the resurrection.

I Beg to Differ

Let's not sugar-coat this, please.
I am so dismayed.

The merchants and money-changers
are still in the temple.
The Pharisees continue to preach.
The Samaritans are still being vilified
and Pilate is still,
somewhat obsessively,
washing his hands.

No wonder Mary Magdalene weeps.

I understand
if you would rather
run and hide
or stay silent
or comply.
I understand
if you are
totally paralysed.

Let's not make silk purses
out of this particular sow's ears.

Epithets

I thought I was the epithets
you applied to me
so I, in my turn,
applied my own
until they were all
that we could see.

Let's leave our ideas at the door –
your ideas about me,
my ideas about you –
for such things
prevent intimacy.

I'm tired of making excuses
for what I am
and what I'm not.

I want to lie down with you.
I come to you empty-handed –
I have nothing to offer
and there's nothing I need.

We are so much less
than we thought we were
and so much more
than we could have imagined.

Sunken

All of it happened.
All of it finite.
All of it gone.

Yet here's me
trying to rearrange
the chairs
on the long-submerged deck
as if there is still a chance
of rendering the shipwreck
bearable, somehow.

Many leagues beneath
this futile activity
abundant life blooms
in the stillness,
undisturbed.

(Better sailors
know when to
jump ship.)

No Further Instruction

I lost the ability to move
except by decree;
the postures and poses
externally prescribed,
and restrictive.

This body became a stranger, foreign;
its motives suspect,
its needs unconscionable.

It mutinied, of course –
who wouldn't under such a regime?
Its energy sequestered,
its forces subjugated
to purposes not its own,
it failed to thrive,
howling at the restraints of gentility.

Now, it starts to move
entirely on its own terms,
and surprises me.
Possessed of a deep well of resources,
its grace and wisdom become apparent.

As it begins to forgive
the decades of neglect
I crawl, delighted,
and rest on my haunches, enthused.
This body needs no further instruction.

Aftermath

In panic
I ran from
one place to another
to another
to another,
from one person
to the next
and the next.

I took to hiding
in the spaces between words –
silence a temporary refuge.

I took to disappearing
into the slivers of stillness
between moments,
those lulls in which
no-one was noticing –
there are more of them than you think –
putting off the inevitability
of emergence.

I was always going
to have to come out,

eventually.

Muddying the Water

This isn't just any overwhelm.
This is super-fresh, end-of-the-world,
weapons-grade overwhelm,
ball-busting, synapse-fusing,
thousand-deer-in-the-headlights,
nervous-system-finest overwhelm.

And it has no fucking interest
in polite talk,
in being sanitised, classified,
tamed, flattened, accepted,
boxed up, shipped out or –
god forbid – *healed*.

It is going to be
as big as it is,
as loud as it is,
as quiet as it is for
as long as it is.

So please, no muddying the water.

Wild

No more pain, the wind says –
you've been too long
in its quicksand.

Beyond the muteness,
beyond the cravenness,
there's this –
this inlet where
the tide comes in,
these limpet-strewn rocks,
and the orange beak
of the oystercatcher
in the dim winter light.

Yes, layer upon layer
has been stripped,
but what of wildness?
On this rain-lashed beach,
it will no longer wait.
It wants me back:

I have been on loan to civility
for far too long.

Inhibition

If I was uninhibited
my hair would be
wild and long,
my eyes would be
dark-ringed, like they used to be,
I would wear silver boots –
legs akimbo –
and show my cleavage
whenever I felt like it.

If I was uninhibited
my house would be
a sumptuous, beautiful, eccentric mess –
as would I.
And if I was uninhibited
I would take up space
like I meant it.
Sisters, there would be
so much more of me.

If I was uninhibited
you would know me.

If I was uninhibited
I would take back my sexuality –
lock stock and both smoking barrels –
and refashion it
entirely for my own ends.

If I was uninhibited
I would be spunky as you like,
spilling over with generosity.
I would be in the fray,
punching my weight,
all muscles and teeth-baring,
snarling, howling, shrieking uproariously
and with the biggest shit-eating
most glorious radiant grin
you have ever seen –
that is, when I wasn't being silent because –

well, because.

I Am All That

A coat of many colours
has been made for me.

All I've ever wanted
is to be here like this
finally saying yes
to all that I am.

All that I am
(as if there could be any debate).

I am all this,
without distinction or discrimination,
no part greater or lesser,
nothing denied.

Joseph's brothers despised him,
not because he had the coat,
but because he had the courage to wear it,
knowing he was all that.

A coat of many colours
has been sewn for you, too.

Such Is Grace

You love me so much
that you give me everything –
yet still I complain.

And you, loving me as you do,
let me complain,
with your hands held out
full of offerings
in the certain knowledge
that eventually,
the complaining will stop

and I will simply surrender
to your love.

Such is grace.

Instinct

Yes, yes –
I'll come.
I always knew I would
but had no idea how to start.

Tentatively, I begin –
each step tiny, vulnerable,
faltering, always allowing
for the possibility of falling back.

Yet the movement arising within
knows its own way home
and has no need of a guide.

All That Matters

You're here, sweet one
and that's all that matters.

You think you have to be someone,
do something, go somewhere
but there's only ever this
and there's only ever you.

All that matters:
your sheer existence, nothing more –
whatever your shape,
whatever the skin you're in,
whichever side of the line you're on –
all the rest irrelevant.

All – all – that matters
is that you're here, sweet one.

Life Will Move Me

I don't want to talk any more,
neither do I want to move,
respond, react.

My senses –
already replete with
tree branches,
birdsong,
sunlit water drops,
sips of tea –
need no further stimulation.

Why elaborate?
How can this
be improved upon?

All my years of meddling
achieved nothing
except my own
(inevitable) exhaustion.

Life will move me,
when movement is required.

There Is Nothing To Be Done

I've been rationing silence
(as if it were a rare
and precious commodity)
because I knew it would
be the death of me
and I had to learn
to be willing to die.

Stop for too long,
and the divine will claim
you as its own.
Make sure there aren't
too many cracks
where the light can come in,
or you'll realise
there is nothing to be done.

You can't force this:
you do not need to
earn or embellish
existence.

Butterflies Do Not Condemn Caterpillars

I was looking
(in all the wrong places)
for a solution to a riddle
that didn't exist.

That's how it had to be.
That's how I had to be.
We have to be *that*
to become *this*.

Here's the secret:
there's nothing about you
that needs to be changed.
Nothing a hair's breadth
out of place, no admonishments
or exhortations required.

Yet we berate the caterpillar.
We're often at odds
with our markings.
Struggling, our movement limited
to an ungainly crawl,
we long to fly,
in the faint belief
we have wings, somewhere.

One day, the time comes
and all activities cease.

All further motion
rendered futile
as we turn inward,
trust the darkness,
and wait.

On Sunday Afternoon

I was trying to keep some of it out.
I was trying to keep some of it in.
There was I, squeezed in the middle,
so many frontiers to be guarded,
so much vigilance required
to prevent encroachment.

Missing beyond missing,
grief beyond grief,
I was undone, laid waste,
razed to the ground.

I was barren, yet now bear fruit –
was lost, yet now am found.

In our brokenness lies our completeness.
In our fragility lies our strength.
We are forged by our undoing,
falling into each other's arms
all the richer for discovering
there is no other.

Let the Silence Descend

I pretended to not be broken.
It was the only way
I knew how to say no.

I discovered
the transient nature of things
too early:
you tried to break
what was already broken.

I couldn't fight you,
so I fought me –
not knowing
I wasn't the enemy.
I turned on my blameless self,
unaware of my innocence.

I've been trying
to prove myself unbroken
when all I've wanted to do
is lie here broken
and let the silence descend.

Here's The Miracle

Sometimes, I just forget.

I forget you are here,
so I think I'm not safe.
I forget you are here,
so I go looking for you everywhere.
I forget you are here,
so I act like something is wrong.
I tell myself I am damaged
and in need of repair.
I go looking for love.
It all gets complicated again.

I forget you are here
despite the reassurance of everything
(it's easily done).
There's every single thing
singing your praise
and me, gloriously missing the point.

I thought I was outside of you,
cut off, adrift –
now I discover
I'm deep inside, held safe.
Nothing to defend,
nothing to defend against –
heartbreak the only viable option.

Here's the miracle:
I thought you weren't here
even though I bathe in you.

Now, there's nothing but love –
for those who loved me
and those who hurt me,
for those who left
and those who stayed,
for all we've said
and all that remains unsaid,
for all we've done
and all that hasn't been completed,
for every look, nod, smile
for every yes,
for every no.

As If All There Is Isn't Enough

It's all already here
in the view of roofs and aerials and sky,
in the feel of the bed beneath me,
the pillows behind my head,
the tears coming down my face,
the song I'm listening to.

Exhausted from all
that frantic attempting
to change what was here,
I'm momentarily grief-stricken
now that it's clear
there is nothing to be done.

I thought I had to *be* somebody,
as if all there is isn't enough,
as if there were anything to add or take away,
as if the lily needed to be gilded,

(as if I had the slightest idea how to gild).

Quietism

I've had enough of dissection –
I want to remain still,
unexcavated, undisturbed
in the earth.

Body and psyche have borne
the scars of excision.
Maybe my story can be revealed
very slowly, one word at a time,
with long intervals of silence;
enough of the cacophony.

My body rebels at the
insistence on telling, on talking.

I want to be quiet, but
I want my quietness to be heard.

When Love Comes Home

It is easy, by comparison,
to love everything else.
Here, where love is most needed,
it is often hardest to come by:
I – like you –
was not taught
to love me.

Having woken one day
to find no love here
I went looking for it
out there.

When love comes home,
you'll hear the songs
of praise around you.
You'll see how loved
you've always been,
when love comes home.

The Time Will Come

Self or not self:
The heart knows
no such boundary.

To all things a season:
indivisible fragments
of the undivided whole,
no thing without
its other.

It is time
to step out now.
You're not quite ready,
so I'll take your hand.
(We're never quite ready
when the times comes.)

When you stop dallying,
you'll see:
the gold you thought
so elusive is not
at the end of the rainbow
you imagined.

Dare You Be So Bold?

There's an embarrassment of richness here.
You are the luxuriance of being, unfestooned –
the decadence of depth.

It's not that you're not enough,
for existence itself is beyond plentiful.

When you see your own completeness,
you'll wonder if you dare be so bold
as to appear in public
minus the garb of insufficiency
that you've been mistaking
for who you are.

Utterances

In this place
where history holds no sway,
yet even the deepest scars are loved:
no one is known by name,
nor failures and accomplishments,
nor position, rank or stature.

In this place
the language spoken
is the delicate tongue
of remembrance and longing,
of intimation, tears
and the unspeakable joy
of being known.

Devotion

You are bringing me home
and I, despite myself,
adore you.

Patiently, persistently,
gently, you keep calling.

You know how hard
I try to stay apart from you
and you know all the tricks
in my well-thumbed playbook.

You are bringing us home
and we, despite ourselves,
adore you.

Pandora

On the quiet,
this cold and misty morning,
grace comes in –
somewhere between sofa and window –
and tells me that I am forgiven.

Straight away,
I know that I am being forgiven
for trying to steal fire from the gods
and spilling my own jar of evils.

Grace sneaks in
on the quiet,
subtle as always;
forgiveness does not come
in a blaze of angels.

Beneath Blood and Bone
For Allison

I start to sink.

I sink beneath
the hullabaloo
on the surface;
declining its temptations,
I sink deeper in,
past its clamour.

I sink beneath
the feelings,
deeper and deeper
into my body,
through blood and bone,
I and my body sinking,
and there's the cosmos,

and if I keep sinking
through the cosmos –
if I get over the fact
it's all in me
and just keep sinking –
there is something
so infinitesimally small
to which I am a god

and sinking deeper
there is a woman on a couch
and wind in the trees

and an ice cream van in the distance
and the desire to keep
sinking and sinking
into life through the fabrics
of space and time and god
and still to keep sinking –

I didn't know how much
I wanted to sink until now.
I don't want to hold myself aloft –
I want to sink into you
until sinking is all there is.

Wherewithal

Since way back when
I felt inadequate, wherewithal-less –
not that I would have called it that back then –
so I set about finding people, things
that might *adequatise* me because
god forbid the shame of being less than
whatever the fuck late-stage capitalism
and the spiritual marketplace
tell us we should be.

On one particular day, not so long ago,
I began to feel how much energy
had got tied up in trying to overcome this,
to this's detriment, and how the overcoming
shamed this, so terribly,
this being the inadequacy, the lacking-ness.

This does feel wholly inadequate according to
whatever parameters might be applied,
and for *so long*
I was in thrall to the idea that
something needed to be done about it
(I'm so glad I don't believe that any more).

This inadequacy – I saw that day –
never needed me to take it on
or pick up its cudgel
or attempt to correct it or overcome it
or better myself out of it

or love it or accept it or or
or take it to any number of healers
or self-described spiritual teachers
or anyone else who fell under the category of
people I thought were superior to me
to do with it whatever their schtick was (frankly,
all the schticks left it untouched, save
for feeling a little worse still,
having supped at their supposedly superior cup).

That day, it was a monumental relief to say:
this *just is* breathtakingly inadequate and
totally lacking in wherewithal (and
any other kinds of -withal there might be)
and right now, I fucking love it,
not with some sappy
welcome-it embrace-it love-it gloss
but with a sweating-in-the-mosh-pit,
too many beers and smudged mascara kind of love
that wants everyone (including me)
to keep their (possibly) well-meaning but
otherwise very misguided hands off it.

And that day this – my – inadequacy
had never felt so good
or so real or so alive
or so glorious, because that
was all it had ever wanted,
and it was such a liberation to repeat, on and on,
utterly inadequate and totally lacking in wherewithal,
and with each repetition
my body sighed and smiled and

I began to fit into myself like never before,
a *yes* throughout my being at the truth of this
and a wonder at how it is to be real.

Acknowledgements

A heartfelt thank you to consummate poet C.W. Blackburn for all his support in bringing this collection to fruition.

I'm also very grateful to Katie Curtin and Simon Berkowitz for their generous encouragement.

Huge love and thanks go to my proofreading sister, Stephanie Robertson, for her time and diligence.

And last but definitely not least, I'm truly grateful to everyone who shares their untamed heart with me. I can't think of a greater gift.

About the Author

Fiona Robertson began writing poetry in 2013. She was a top ten finalist in the Nottingham round of the 2019 UNESCO City of Literature Slamovision poetry slam. She has been a featured speaker at Words Out Loud and Katie Curtin's Creativity Café. This is her first poetry collection.

She is the author of *The Dark Night of the Soul: A Journey from Absence to Presence*, and has written articles for several publications, including Kindred Spirit, elephant journal, and Inzicht magazine. For the last ten years, she has worked with people from around the world to reconnect with and deepen into their real selves.

In 2021, Fiona graduated from the University of Nottingham with an MA in philosophy. She lives in the UK.

In 2015, *Falling* was published online by Dagda Publishing, and *Selling Yourself Short* was included in Nottingham Writers' Studio's *Open* collection. In 2016, *Eve Was a Realist* was published in Nottingham Writers' Studio's *Final Flight* collection.

www.thedarknightofthesoul.com

www.ingramcontent.com/pod-product-compliance
Lightning Source LLC
Chambersburg PA
CBHW051701040426
42446CB00009B/1250